P9-DGH-297

RANDOM MARVEL MOVIE FACTS YOU PROBABLY DON'T KNOW

(352 Fun Facts and Secret Trivia from the Marvel Cinematic Universe)

by: Mariah Caitlyn

All rights reserved. No part of this publication may be reproduced, distributed, or transmitted in any form or by any means, including photocopying, recording, or other electronic or mechanical methods, without the prior written permission of the publisher, except in the case of brief quotations embodied in critical reviews and certain other noncommercial uses permitted by copyright law.

Edited by Tom F. Whitehall

Edition: 2

Fun Facts and Secret Trivia

Iron Man (2008) 4

The Incredible Hulk (2008)...11

Iron Man 2 (2010) 17

Thor (2011) 24

Captain America: The First Avenger (2011) 30

The Avengers (2012) 34

Iron Man 3 (2013) 41

Thor: The Dark World (2013) 44

Captain America: The Winter Soldier (2014) 49

Guardians of the Galaxy (2014) 53

Avengers: Age of Ultron (2015) 60

Ant-Man (2015) 66

Captain America: Civil War (2016) 71

Iron Man (2008)

1. When Phil Coulson gives Tony Stark his pre-written statement for the final press conference, he says the official statement will be that Tony was on the island of Attilan. In the comic books, Attilan is the ancestral home of the Inhumans, a highly-advanced race of superhumans.

2. Obadiah Stane has a line where he tells Tony Stark "We're iron mongers, we make weapons." Stane's supervillain name is the Iron Monger.

3. According to Jon Favreau, it was very difficult to choose the first villain for Iron Man to face, since almost all of the villains he fights in the comic books are very powerful, and it wouldn't be a realistic movie if Tony Stark creates the Iron Man suit in the first act, and battles a near-god in the second act.

4. In one of the original drafts, Obadiah Stane survived the final battle and it was planned he would re-appear in *Iron Man 2*.

5. At the end of the movie, Agent Coulson creates a cover story where Iron Man is employed by Tony Stark to act as his bodyguard. Stark dismisses it as "pretty flimsy." This is exactly how his cover maintained for years in the comic books.

6. Sounds effects from the classic arcade game Space Invaders, were used to create some of J.A.R.V.I.S.'s beeps and boops.

7. Rachael McAdams turned down the role of Pepper Potts because she was busy with other projects.

8. The secret scene with Nick Fury was shot with a skeleton crew and the only actors Samuel L. Jackson and Robert Downey Jr. had seen the script. It was a surprise to most of the cast and crew who worked on the movie when they saw it in the theaters.

9. Sam Rockwell auditioned to play Tony Stark. He ended up landing the role of a villain in *Iron Man 2.* Timothy Olyphant also auditioned to play the role of Tony.

10. When Tony is programming the Iron Man suit's boot-up sequence in the cave, the computer language you see is the C language.

11. In the final battle with the Iron Monger, Iron Man was supposed to crash an Audi R8 into his legs and it would split in two, except the car was so well built it wouldn't break properly and the scene had to be re-written.

12. Right before the final press conference, Tony Stark is reading the newspaper with an amateur photograph of Iron Man on the cover. The picture is part of a video, shot by movie-set trespassers hiding in a bush during early filming. The video appeared on the internet before the movie was finished filming and the producers decided to use it as a marketing stunt.

13. If *Iron Man* had been as big a flop as *John Carter,* Marvel Studios would have gone bankrupt. Everything was riding on the success of *Iron Man.*

14. In the scene where Pepper discovers Tony removing the damaged Iron Man armor, you can see a prototype of Captain America's shield sitting on a workbench.

15. Gwyneth Paltrow said she only took the role of Pepper Potts because all her scenes were to be shot at the studio 15 minutes from her house. At the time of filming she had two very young children and she didn't want to leave them. In an early draft, she had some scenes in Afghanistan, but they were cut.

16. In 1999, Quentin Tarantino turned down an offer to write and direct an *Iron Man* movie.

17. To prepare for his role as Obadiah Stane, Jeff Bridges read all the Iron Man comics he could find that had the Iron Monger in them.

18. The *Iron Man* script was created by combining two drafts from completely different screenwriters and giving it to a third screenwriter to polish. But when filming started the script still wasn't complete and much of the dialogue ended up being written by the actors.

19. While Tony Stark and James Rhodes are walking through the casino in Vegas, you can hear a jazz version of the 1960s Iron Man cartoon theme song.

20. In one scene. Obadiah Stane plays on the piano a musical piece written by 18th-century composer Antonio Salieri. Salieri is said to have murdered Mozart, somewhat of a parallel of the relationship between Stane and Stark in the movie.

21. The scene where Tony flies too high and his suit stalls because of ice build-up, was meant to be a parallel to the classic story of Icarus, who flew too close to the sun and his had his wings melt.

22. The movie began development in 1990 but kept getting postponed.

23. The Stark Industries logo is similar to that of Lockheed Martin, co-developer of the F-22 Raptor, the fighter plane which is seen in the movie.

24. Paul Bettany recorded all off his J.A.R.V.I.S. voice-over scenes in less than two hours.

25. Robert Downey Jr. credits Burger King with helping him get off drugs in 2003. That idea what worked into the final scene where Tony sits down to eat the burger.

26. *Iron Man* the only Marvel movie not to feature any choreographed martial arts fight scenes.

27. J.A.R.V.I.S. stands for "Just A Rather Very Intelligent System."

28. To prepare for the role of James Rhodes, Terrence Howard visited the Nellis Air Force Base. He ate with the men and watched the helicopter and fighter jet power-up and power-down sequences.

29. The pilots in the F-22 jets are referred to as Whiplash 1 and Whiplash 2. Whiplash is the name of the villain in *Iron Man 2*.

30. When filming the final press conference, the extras were told it was a dream sequence so they wouldn't spoilt it on the internet.

31. Hugh Jackman was offered the role of Tony Stark but turned it down because he was already too well known as the character Wolverine.

32. Some of Tony's mannerisms were based off video footage of SpaceX founder, Elon Musk.

33. Obadiah Stane brings Tony pizza from New York City in a box marked: RAY'S. Ray's is a famous chain of pizza joints real life.

34. During filming, a tank accidentally ran over a $4,000 Aaton 35mm camera.

35. The montage of Tony Stark's life story and has real-life photos of a young Robert Downey Jr. and his real-life father, Robert Downey Sr.

The Incredible Hulk (2008)

1. Though the final battle scene is set in Harlem, Manhattan, the film was shot in Canada, with the initial showdown between Hulk and Abomination being filmed on Yonge Street, in Toronto, Canada. Several iconic Yonge Street businesses are visible in the shot, including Sam the Record Man, and the Zanzibar Tavern.

2. A scene where a depressed Bruce Banner travels to the Arctic to commit suicide was featured in many movie trailers, but it was cut from the final film as to not upset younger viewers.

3. In the final scene of the movie, General Ross is drinking a cocktail called The Incredible Hulk. It is a green-colored alcoholic drink made by mixing equal parts of the fruit liqueur Hpnotiq and Hennessy-brand cognac, then poured over ice cubes.

4. The director, Louis Letterier originally wanted Mark Ruffalo to play the role of Bruce Banner, but Marvel insisted the role go to Edward Norton. Mark Ruffalo plays The Hulk in *The Avengers, Avengers: Age of Ultron,* and is cast to play him the 2017 film, *Thor: Ragnarok.*

5. When Bruce Banner is in Hulk form he has three lines of dialogue, "Leave Me Alone", "Hulk Smash", and "Betty." The lines were recorded by Lou Ferrigno, the actor who played Hulk in the late 1970s.

6. William Hurt accepted the role of General 'Thunderbolt' Ross because he was a huge fan of the Hulk comic books. He plays the same character in Captain America: Civil War (due out May 6th, 2016) although he is now the Secretary of State.

7. Edward Norton re-wrote many of his own scenes and also directed these scenes himself, but he was not given writing credit by the WGA. This is because most of Norton's changes were dialogue-based. Had he significantly changed the plot or structure of the film we would have received credit.

8. Special effects artists used footage of NFL linebackers to animate the bulky movements of Hulk and Abomination.

9. The Hercules aircraft seen at the beginning of the movie is actually a Canadian Air Force plane and was flown by Canadian pilots. It was painted over to look like an US Air Force plane.

10. The film is tinted with the exact shade of green as the Hulk's skin.

11. Edward Norton was a huge fan of Hulk, but initially turned down the lead as he had concerns over how the film would turn out. But after meeting director Louis Leterrier and the team at Marvel he signed on. He liked their vision for a huge series of comic book movies, though he has not appeared in a Marvel movie since...

12. The Hulk's design was based on comic book artist Dale Keown's work. He has said, "The Hulk, being beyond perfect, has zero grams of fat, is all chiseled, and is defined by his muscle and strength so he's like a tank."

13. *The Incredible Hulk* was the fourth film where Edward Norton's character had a deranged alter-ego. The other movies were: Primal Fear (1996), Fight Club (1999) and The Score (2001).

14. Louis Leterrier directed a lot of the movie with a broken foot.

15. Louis Leterrier wanted to direct *Iron Man* but he was never offered the position.

16. Liv Tyler accepted her role in this film without ever having read the script. She's since casually mentioned that her policy in that matter has changed, and she now reads all the scripts before she accepts a role.

17. The military base mentioned in the film was Fort Johnson. It was named after Kenneth Johnson, the writer, director, and producer of the original The Incredible Hulk (1978) television series.

18. Abomination was supposed to return as a minor villain in *Avengers: Age of Ultron,* but he was cut from the script.

19. Edward Norton removed Bruce Banner's sidekick Rick Jones from the script when he did the first re-write.

20. Norton wrote a small part exclusively for Michael Kenneth Williams (Omar Little, from *The Wire*) because he was a big fan of his work on the show.

21. In one scene, Betty purchases Bruce some purple pants to wear. In the comic books, the Hulk usually has purple pants on.

22. Ray Stevenson was on the short-list to play the villain, Emil Blonsky. He would later play Volstagg in the Thor films. The role of Emil Blonsky went to Tim Roth.

23. *The Incredible Hulk* was half reboot and half sequel, and has been referred to many film critics as a "requel."

24. Lou Ferrigno recommended Edward Norton for the part of Bruce Banner.

Iron Man 2 (2010)

1. The rooftop where Tony Stark and Pepper Potts kiss at the end of the movie is an apartment building looking over Flushing Meadows, the area where director Jon Favreau lived as a child.

2. The medals presented to James Rhodes and Tony Stark at the end of the film are real military medals. Rhodes is awarded the Meritorious Service Medal, and Stark is awarded the Distinguished Service Medal.

3. The maps and locations on the monitors in the Shield headquarters at the end of the film correspond to characters and events from the Marvel comic books. The location in Africa is a reference to Black Panther (who lives in the fictional country of Wakanda.) Other locations refer to Thor, Captain America, and The Hulk.

4. In the first draft, Whiplash escapes at the end of the movie. In the second draft, he died at the end of the movie. In the final version his fate is left unknown in case he is needed to play a role as minor villain in one of The Avengers' movies.

5. In *Captain America: Winter Soldier* it is revealed that Senator Stern is a member of HYDRA, which explains why the character was trying so hard to take Tony Stark's technology in *Iron Man 2*.

6. Stan Lee can be seen playing the part of Larry King. Though he has a cameo role in every Marvel movie, it is the first time his cameo was a named person, and a famous one at that!

7. Scarlett Johansson dyed her hair red before she was offered the part of Black Widow because she really wanted to play the part.

8. The DJ at Tony's birthday party was DJ AM (a remixer and musician known for performing at private celebrity events.) He died from a drug overdose shortly after filming of the movie had finished. The film is dedicated to him in the credits.

9. Mickey Rourke's Oscar-nominated performance in *The Wrestler* was the reason he was offered the part of Ivan Vanko.

10. The US Marshal who serves Tony his subpoena is played by Kate Mara. Tony asks her where she's from and she replies, "Bedford" which is where Kata Mara was born.

11. Tony Stark's racecar in Monaco was supposed to be painted bright red (like the Iron Man suit), but Robert Downey Jr. insisted on driving a blue and white car as he felt the red car was cheesy.

12. Sam Rockwell accepted the role of Justin Hammer without reading the script. This was because he was friends with both the director and screenwriter and trusted their skills.

13. Because he is so technologically illiterate, Mickey Rourke has stated that the hardest part of playing Ivan Vanko was pretending he was a computer wizard.

14. Natalie Rushman (played by Scarlett Johansson) has the same initials as Natasha Romanoff. Natalie Rushman is also a cover identity that Black Widow uses in the comic books.

15. The photo Tony Stark sees in his research of Ivan Vanko being arrested is an actual photo of actor Mickey Rourke being arrested on a drugs charge.

16. Scarlett Johansson spent months doing extensive physical training to prepare for her role as Black Widow. She maintained her exercise routine even while filming the movie.

17. Mickey Rourke wrote his character's bird and gold teeth into the script and paid for both because he didn't want his character to be one-dimensional.

18. When speaking with Senator Stern, Tony Stark mentions that he would gladly accept the position of Secretary of Defense, an event that actually occurs in the comic books.

19. Mickey Rourke prepared for the role of Whiplash by visiting with real inmates in a Russian jail.

20. Don Cheadle thought Iron Man was a robot before seeing the 2008 movie.

21. *Iron Man 2* was Jon Favreau's first sequel as both an actor and director.

22. A tattoo of Loki had to be digitally removed from Mickey Rourke's neck during post-production because the producer's felt it might confuse fans into thinking there was a connection between Whiplash and the Norse God (who was to be featured in *Thor* and *The Avengers*.)

23. When Tony Stark asks Natalie Rushman "Do you even speak Latin?" she replies with "Fallaces sunt rerum species," meaning "The appearances of things are deceptive."

24. In the Marvel movies, Scarlett Johansson's character is employed by Samuel L. Jackson's character. They had the same relationship in *The Spirit* except they were both villains.

25. In the Chinese version of the film, references to Russia and every instance of the word "Russian" have been removed. No reason has ever been given.

26. The layout and buildings of the Stark Expo 1974 were based on the 1964/65 New York World's Fair.

27. Tony Stark refers to the suitcase with is Iron Man suit in it "the football," a reference to the briefcase with nuclear launch codes that always accompanies the American President. "The football" has been used in many movies and TV shows (like *24*) as prominent plot device.

28. Terrence Howard dropped out of *Iron Man 2* because his character (James Rhodes) had very few lines in the original draft. He was also going to be paid significantly less. After he was replaced by Don Cheadle, the script was changed and the character was given more lines. There was also many rumors that director Jon Favreau did not like working with Howard.

29. Emily Blunt was the first choice to play the character of Black Widow, but had to pull out of the project due to scheduling conflicts with *Gulliver's Travels*.

30. Mickey Rourke has mentioned in several interviews that several of Ivan Vanko's scenes that would have made him look more like a misunderstood/sympathetic villain were cut from the movie.

31. Justin Hammer's factory is really Elon Musk's SpaceX facility. The extras in the background are actual SpaceX employees.

32. Justin Theroux was brought on to re-write the script at the instance of Robert Downey Jr. who liked his work on *Tropic Thunder*.

33. Al Pacino was heavily considered for the role of Justin Hammer.

Thor (2011)

1. The Norwegian village in the flashback scene is the same village the Nazis and Red Skull attack when they steal the tesseract in *Captain America: The First Avenger*.

2. In Norse legend, Loki was the God of Fire, not a Frost Giant.

3. The post-credit scene in *Thor* was directed by Joss Whedon, the director of *The Avengers*.

4. Samuel L. Jackson described his frequent Nick Fury scene at the end of credits as "connective tissue to *The Avengers*."

5. Jessica Biel auditioned for the role of Sif but was not offered the job.

6. In the first draft of the script, the "Einstein-Rosen Bridge" was simply called "the wormhole," but the producers felt it was too close to the terminology used in Star Trek and Stargate.

7. Several scenes that dealt with Loki's being abandoned by Laufey were cut from the final script to make Loki less sympathetic.

8. Thor's costume has elements from every unique costume from all the comic books.

9. *Thor* had been in development hell since the early 1990s. Sam Raimi was originally supposed to direct it, but went on to direct the Spiderman movies instead.

10. The main town in the film was a set constructed exclusively for the film. On the water tower you can see a sign that says, "Home of the Vikings."

11. Mjölnir means "grinder" in ancient Norse.

12. Stellan Skarsgård, the actor who plays Dr. Selvig is an atheist and not does not believe in any of the Norse gods or myths.

13. Chris Hemsworth spent six months working out and eating lots of protein to bulk up for the movie. He put on so much muscle that his costumes all had to be remade before shooting as the designers did not expect him to get *that* big.

14. Anthony Hopkins accepted the role of Odin because of the interesting dynamics surrounding the father/son relationship. He wasn't even a comic book fan. Stan Lee expressed interest in playing Odin, but was happy with the selection of Anthony Hopkins.

15. In one scene, Thor enters a pet shop and demands a horse. Jane later picks him up in her truck, Pinzgauer 716. The Pinzgauer is an Austrian breed of horse.

16. To prepare for his role as Loki, Tom Hiddleston trained at capoeira school. Capoeira a Brazilian martial art that combines elements of music, dance, and acrobatics. He also went on a diet and lost a lot of weight so his lean demeanor would serve as a contrast with his muscular on-screen brother, Thor.

17. To prepare for his role of Heimdall, Idris Elba read every comic book he could find with his character in it.

18. Chris Hemsworth's brother Liam also auditioned for the role of Thor. Other notable actors that also audtioned were: Charlie Hunnam, Tom Hiddleston, and Alexander Skarsgård. Brad Pitt and Daniel Craig were given an opportunity to audition but both declined the offer.

19. Laufey the Frost Giant's makeup took more than five hours to apply.

20. Jim Carry turned down the role of Loki.

21. The film hired several physicists who were tasked with making the science dialogue as realistic as possible.

22. To prepare for his role as Thor, Chris Hemsworth spent months training with a former Navy SEAL. In one scene, Agent Coulson asks Thor if he had been trained by special forces.

23. Walt Simonson (a comic book writer/artist who worked on many popular Thor comic books) has a cameo appearance in the banquet scene at the end of the film. He can be seen sitting between Volstagg and Sif.

24. Jaimie Alexander (Sif) was on the wrestling team in high school, so she did not need much training for the fight scenes.

25. Chris Hemsworth worked as construction worker before he was an actor, and was quite familiar with using big hammers.

26. Another Thor comic book writer, Joseph Michael Straczynski, is one of the first people to attempt to lift Mjölnir out of the crater.

27. The space images in the credits were based off images from the Hubble Space Telescope and took more than a year to create.

Captain America: The First Avenger (2011)

1. During Captain America's war bond drive, the tank burning in the background of the black-and-white film is an M5 Stuart tank painted with German markings. This is historically accurate because it was almost impossible to capture an enemy tank without destroying it, so American tanks had to be painted with German markings for films and propaganda pieces.

2. The final scene was filmed on location in New York City's Times Square. Black Widow (Scarlett Johansson) was supposed to be the nurse who wakes him up but the script was changed.

3. When Bucky and Steve visit the World Fair at the beginning of the film, Bucky says, "We're going to the future." At the end of the movie, Steve Rogers is frozen in ice and wakes up in the future.

4. Rosamund Pike (Amy in *Gone* Girl) auditioned for the role of Peggy Carter but was not offered the job. Emily Blunt turned down an offer to play Peggy.

5. Joe Johnston was chosen to direct the film because of his work on *The Rocketeer* and *October Sky*, two films that took place around the same time period as *Captain America: The First Avenger*.

6. Dane Cook auditioned for the role of Captain America. So did Sebastian Stan, but he landed the role of Bucky.

7. The design of Red Skull's flying fortress at the end of the film was inspired by a large plane in the Nintendo 64 video game Aero Fighters Assault.

8. At the end of the film, Howard Stark finds the tesseract and creates some blueprints for a structure. These blueprints can be seen in *Iron Man 2*.

9. Red Skull was deformed by the super-soldier serum just like Abomination in *The Incredible Hulk*.

10. In the first draft, Baron von Strucker was a sidekick of Red Skull but he was removed so he could be used in *Avengers: Age of Ultron*.

11. Hugo Weaving has declined all further offers to play Red Skull because of the difficulty and length of time it took to apply his makeup. He also didn't love the film or the character.

12. When Col. Phillips (Tommy Lee Jones), Peggy, and Captain America are chasing the Hydra plane in Schmidt's car, Phillips presses a red button, with the letter K on it. In the movie *Men in Black*, Tommy Lee Jones' character is named Kay, and he tells Jay (Will Smith) to never touch the red button.

13. Red Skull's real name is Johan Schmidt. Johan Schmidt is the German version of John Smith.

14. More than 10 different shields were created for Captain America and were made out of different materials, depending on what was needed for the shot. When he was throwing the shield, it would usually be plastic or rubber, but when he was putting it on his back it would be made of magnetized metal.

15. The actor who played Adolph Hitler (James Payton) also played Hitler in *The Monuments Men* three years later.

16. The "skinny" version of Steve Rogers was created by digitally placing Chris Evan's head on top of a skinny body double.

17. Hayley Atwell (Peggy Carter) touching Chris Evans' chest as he emerged from the pod after being injected with the super-soldier serum, was improvised, and the surprise on her face is real.

18. The super-soldier serum is not strictly a serum as there are many other processes involved aside from the injection. It is not explained why it works on Steve Rogers but turns other people into monsters.

19. Joss Whedon re-wrote many scenes in *Captain America: The First Avenger* so they would connect better with *The Avengers*. He did not receive any writing credit from the WGA. Joss Whedon has mentioned several times he thinks it's ridiculous that someone can re-write almost every line of dialogue in a movie and not receive credit.

20. In the comic books, the "first" Avengers were Thor, Iron Man, Wasp, and Ant-Man.

21. Chris Evans turned down the role of Captain America three times. In the end, Robert Downey Jr. convinced him to do it by telling him if it was a hit then he would be able to star in any movie he wanted.

The Avengers (2012)

1. Edward Norton was replaced by Mark Ruffalo as The Hulk because Edward made too many changes to his dialogue in *The Incredible Hulk*. He also refused to help promote the movie.

2. On the Helicarrier, a S.H.I.E.L.D. employee is seen playing Galaga, an alien-invasion video game which parallels the final battle against the Chitauri.

3. A post-credits scene with James Rhodes arriving in the War Machine suit was cut from the final script, and replaced with the "shawarma" scene.

4. In the final battle, much of Stark Tower is destroyed, including the sign that says "Stark Tower." All that remains of the sign is the letter "A." In the sequel, Stark Tower has turns into the Avengers headquarters.

5. Joss Whedon did not approve of Agent Coulson dying. It was a Marvel Executive's idea, and it was unpopular with the fans. Agent Coulson was brought back in the *Agents of S.H.I.E.L.D.* TV series.

6. Several gruesome scenes and sound effects had to be cut from *The Avengers* in order to lower the rating from R to PG-13.

7. Lindsay Lohan auditioned for the role of Maria Hill. So did Jessica Lucas, Morena Baccarin, and Mary Elizabeth Winstead.

8. *The Avengers* was the highest-grossing film of 2012. It was also the first film to bring in more than $200 million within three days (in America.) It was also the first Marvel movie to bring in more than a billion dollars.

9. While Ant-Man and Wasp were founding members of the Avengers team in the comic books, they were cut from the movie so they could get a standalone film.

10. Many scenes that were supposed to be filmed in Michigan were instead filmed in Ohio because many of Michigan's film and television tax credits were ended.

11. Natalie Portman had a cameo scene written for her but she couldn't accept it because she was pregnant and scheduled to have her baby around the time the film was shot.

12. Scarlett Johansson turned down the female lead in *Total Recall* because she was busy with *The Avengers*.

13. Mark Ruffalo's performance of The Hulk is the first time an actor has played both Bruce Banner *and* The Hulk. In all other film and TV adaptations, two actors were used. Special effects artists turned Mark into The Hulk with motion-capture technology.

14. The janitor character who asks Bruce Banner if he is an alien — also played one of the main characters in *Alien*.

15. *The Avengers* held the record for comic book movie with the most number of Oscar nominations until it was beaten by *X-Men: Days of Future Past*.

16. Edward Norton has mentioned he would have passed on *The Avengers* if it was offered to him, because The Hulk was dealing with his anger issues which Edward felt had been resolved in *The Incredible Hulk*, thus his character would have very little character development and end up being boring.

17. The Hulk's computer generated body was modeled after a male stripper. The face was modeled after Mark Ruffalo.

18. Hawkeye as the lowest amount of screen-time in the movie, just under 13 minutes. Captain America had the highest at 37 minutes and 46 seconds.

19. Stark Tower is located where the MetLife Building is in Midtown Manhattan. The bottom part of Stark Tower looks exactly like the MetLife Building.

20. Thor is knocked off the screen twice by The Hulk, and twice by Iron Man, but zero times by Loki or the Chitauri.

21. The scene where The Hulk brings Iron Man back to consciousness by roaring at him was improvised by Mark Ruffalo.

22. Real police officers were hired as extras for the final battle scene to make it as realistic as possible.

23. When the missile is flying over Manhattan, the pilot declares it will explode in two minutes and thirty seconds. Unlike most movies, it actually explodes two minutes and thirty seconds later.

24. This is the first time in film or comic book history The Hulk is shown with chest hair.

25. The German police car skidding on its front end after Loki blasted it was an accident. It was supposed to flip and explode.

26. In the scene soon after Loki is brought aboard the Helicarrier, Tony Stark is be seen wearing a Black Sabbath T-shirt. One of Black Sabbath's most famous songs is called Iron Man.

27. When Robert Downey Jr. and Gwyneth Paltrow were in a scene together, Robert had to wear platform shoes so he would appear taller than her.

28. One night, when the entire cast of the movie was in New York, Chris Evans sent everybody a text-message saying "Assemble" and they all went out and partied.

29. Jeremy Renner received training from Olympic archers to prepare for his role as Hawkeye.

30. In one scene, Bruce Banner explains how he tried to commit suicide in Alaska. This scene was deleted from *The Incredible Hulk*.

31. Almost 30 minutes of Steve Rogers scenes were cut from the film but ended up being used in *Captain America: The Winter Soldier*. They mostly involved Steve Rogers having a hard time adapting to modern life.

32. Shawarma sales in America went through the roof after people saw *The Avengers*. It was already a popular food in Europe, the Middle East, and Canada.

Iron Man 3 (2013)

1. Jon Favreau turned down an offer to direct *Iron Man 3* because of Marvel's constant script changes to *Iron Man 2*. These changes were made to set up future movies in the Marvel universe.

2. In the first draft, Maya Hansen was the main villain, but most of her scenes were cut and she was replaced by The Mandarin.

3. The final line of the movie, "I am Iron Man," is also the final line of the first movie

4. In the scene where Tony and Pepper are discussing the stuffed bunny, you can see a stocking has been put out for J.A.R.V.I.S. and the color scheme matches The Vision's color scheme (red, yellow, and green.) In *The Age of Ultron*, J.A.R.V.I.S. turns into The Vision.

5. Jessica Chastain was cast to play Maya Hansen but dropped out due to scheduling conflicts.

6. *Iron Man 3* is the longest of all three Iron Man movies. It is 130 minutes long. *Iron Man 2* was 124 minutes long, and *Iron Man* was 126 minutes long.

7. *Iron Man 3* is the only Iron Man movie where Nick Fury does not make an appearance. Agent Coulson also does not make an appearance.

8. The director (Shane Black) described the film as a "Tom Clancy thriller."

9. Jude Law expressed interest in the role of Aldrich Killian but the producers felt it would be awkward for the audience, as Jude Law is Robert Downey Jr.'s sidekick in the Sherlock Holmes movies.

10. The official Chinese version of the film includes some scenes deleted from the American version. The scenes feature Chinese actors and characters.

11. *Iron Man 3* is the only Iron Man film not to have AC/DC on the soundtrack.

12. The budget of *Iron Man 3* was initially $140 million, but was bumped up to $200 million after the commercial success of *The Avengers*.

13. The idea for Happy Hogan's favorite television show to be *Downton Abbey* was *Iron Man 2* director Jon Favreau's — who is in real life a big fan of the series.

14. It was Robert Downey Jr.'s Idea that Gwyneth Paltrow's character (Pepper Polts) have a bunch of action scenes.

15. More than an hour of scenes were deleted from the final cut of the movie.

Thor: The Dark World (2013)

1. The director of *Thor: The Dark World* didn't really like the mid-credits scene with The Collector and mentioned that several times in various interviews. He later apologized to James Gunn, the writer/director of the scene and also *Guardians of the Galaxy*.

2. Odin's fate was left purposefully ambiguous, though it is rumored that Anthony Hopkins will return for *Thor: Ragnarok* for at least a few scenes, possibly flashbacks.

3. In one scene, the Aether is identified by the Collector as one of the Infinity Gems. Its red color identifies it as the Gem of Power. It is one of six powerful stones that when combined form the Infinity Gauntlet, which grants the user unlimited power and knowledge.

4. In the first draft, the Aether turns Jane Foster into a supervillain and she destroys the world of the Dark Elves, then returned to Earth to wreak havoc.

5. Natalie Portman was not available to shoot the post-credits scene where Thor and Jane Foster kiss. Instead a body double was used. The body double was Chris Hemsworth's actual wife, actress Elsa Pataky.

6. To shoot the cameo scene where Loki impersonates Captain America, Tom Hiddleston dressed up in full Captain America costume and acted out the full scene. Using the footage, Chris Evans imitated Tom Hiddleston's imitation of himself. This was done to make it as realistic as possible, since even you were to change your appearance, you wouldn't be able to replicate someone's facial expressions and movement quirks unless you had studied them.

7. Odin's throne room is built on the same stage that the last scene in *Star Wars: A New Hope* (the award ceremony scene) was shot. It is one of the largest stages in movie business and located in Surrey, England.

8. The prologue was directed by Tim Miller, the director of Deadpool. Every character except for Malekith, Kurse and Bo are CGI. This is because the Night Elf costumes were too movement-restricting for realistic combat.

9. Producer Kevin Feige described this movie as "The Empire Strikes back of the Thor saga." Many crew members referred to the Dark Elves as "stormtroopers."

10. Just under 11,000 prop weapons were used in the creation of this film.

11. Idris Elba (Heimdall) did not enjoy working on this movie because the script was constantly being rewritten and required many reshoots. He described it as "torture."

12. In an early draft, the big villain was the fire demon Surtur, but that was scrapped.

13. Tom Hiddleston wanted to direct the film but was passed over due to his lack of experience.

14. Kenneth Branagh turned down of offer to direct *Thor: The Dark World* because he was busy working on *Jack Ryan: Shadow Recruit*.

15. Mads Mikkelsen turned down an offer to play the role of Malekith because he was busy working on *Hannibal*.

16. In the first Thor movie, Chris Hemsworth wore a wig. For *Thor: The Dark World* he chose to spend a year growing out his hair.

17. In Norse mythology, the einherjar are the dead who are brought to Valhalla by valkyries. In this film, they are Asgard's city guards.

18. Patty Jenkins was originally slated to direct *Thor: The Dark World* but backed out due to "creative differences" with the Marvel executives. Natalie Portman was very upset and reportedly she wanted to quit the movie, but legally she couldn't get out of her contract. Patty Jenkins has seen been hired to direct *Wonder Woman*. Wonder Woman is a superhero who appears in DC Comics.

19. As the script was constantly being rewritten, many scenes and lines were improvised, including the "banana balls" line, and the scene where Thor hangs his hammer on a coat rack.

20. The stone creature Thor fights is a Kronan, nicknamed the "Stone Men of Saturn." Thor fights a Kronan in his very first comic book.

21. Malekith's make-up took more than six hours to apply.

22. Josh Dallas, who played Fandral in *Thor*, was unable to return to *Thor: The Dark World* due to scheduling conflicts, so he was replaced by Zachary Levi who turned down the role of Fandral in *Thor* because of scheduling conflicts.

23. Director Alan Taylor loved Adewale Akinnuoye-Agbaje's acting so much that he insisted he do all his own stunts. Adewale played the role of Kurse.

24. Like Captain America's shield, more than 30 different versions of Thor's hammer were made from different materials, ranging from light plastic to heavy metal. Different scenes called for different hammers to be used.

25. *Thor: The Dark World* is the first Marvel movie not to be set in the United States.

26. The character of Loki did not appear in the first draft of *Thor: The Dark World*. The script was rewritten after people loved him so much in *The Avengers*.

Captain America: The Winter Soldier (2014)

1. Near the end of the film, when the Helicarriers are selecting their targets for extermination you can see an image of Stark Tower. One of the targets was Tony Stark (Iron Man), and his headshot can be seen in the upper-right corner at timestamp 1:53:44. The Baxter building and the Fantastic Four were also targeted.

2. Chris Evans and Scarlett Johansson improvised most of the dialogue during their "witty banter" type scenes.

3. The events of the film take place in less than three days, which is why there isn't any opportunity for Captain America to call in reinforcements from his other Avenger buddies.

4. In one scene, Black Widow mentions "Operation Paperclip." This was a real operation which saw more than 1,500 German engineers and scientists brought over from Nazi Germany to work on American projects.

5. In an interview, producer Kevin Feige described the film as "A 1970s political thriller masquerading as a big superhero movie."

6. Both Scarlett Johansson and her character, Black Widow, were born in 1984.

7. The Winter Soldier's mask covers the bottom of his face, while Captain America's mask covers the top of his face. This was an intentional decision so show contrast between the two characters.

8. In the comic books, Sam Wilson (Falcon) can telepathically communicate with birds. In the film universe, he's just a normal guy with a suit.

9. Hawkeye (Jeremy Renner) had several scenes in the original draft of this screenplay, but they had to be cut because of (you guessed it) scheduling issues.

10. Kevin Durand auditioned for the role of Crossbones, but he had previously been cast as The Blob in *X-Men Origins: Wolverine.*

11. Batroc the Leaper is played by Georges St-Pierre, a former UFC Welterweight Champion.

12. Despite the film taking place in America and dealing with mostly American issues, the film was more successful *outside* of America.

13. Scarlett Johansson and Chris Evans were both in the movie *Perfect Score*. In this movie, students plot to steal the answers to the SAT. During an interrogation scene in *Captain America: The Winter Soldier,* they mention that "S.H.I.E.L.D. knows everything, even your SAT scores."

14. On Nick Fury's gravestone you can see the epitaph: "The path of the righteous man. Ezekiel 25:17." This is a reference to Samuel L. Jackson's character in Pulp Fiction, would quote the line before killing somebody.

15. Michael Jordan's son, Michael B. Jordan, auditioned for the role of Sam Wilson (Falcon.)

16. This is the first film in the Marvel Cinematic Universe with a scene that shows Nick Fury without his eyepatch on.

17. Joss Whedon directed the mid-credits scene with Baron Strucker, Quicksilver and Scarlet Witch.

18. In the first draft, Dr. Zola transferred his program/consciousness to a robot and escaped the explosion.

19. This film is the first Captain America movie where Steve Rogers does not use a firearm to take out any bad guys. He does, however, still have a pistol strapped to his waist in many scenes.

20. Robert Redford accepted his role because he is almost never offered the part of the villain. He's also said that his grandchildren were huge fans of the Marvel movies and wanted to see him act in one.

21. The document seen in Nick Fury's secret box is a Visa for working in Thailand.

Guardians of the Galaxy (2014)

1. A post-credits scene with Iron Man was cut from this film because Robert Downey Jr. had said he did not plan to play Tony Stark in any fllms after *Captain America: Civil War*. He has since changed his mind and will appear in at least a few more movies, including a new Spiderman movie.

2. Howard the Duck from the post-credits scene is voiced by Seth Green.

3. Also in the post-credits scene you can see Adam Warlock's empty cocoon. Adam Warlock was planned to be actually seen in the post-credits scene, but as his role in a future movie hadn't been confirmed, the scene was cut.

4. Drax is shirtless for the entire movie.

5. In the comic books, Star-Lord becomes the boyfriend of Kitty Pryde (from the X-Men series.)

6. Until Deadpool was released, *Guardians of the Galaxy* was the highest-rated Marvel film.

7. *Guardians of the Galaxy* is the first movie in the Marvel Cinematic Universe that does not have a kissing scene. This is because the movie was initially designed for very young audiences. In fact, in the French version of the film, much of the dialogue was toned down and the adult references removed.

8. In one scene, Rocket makes fun of Star-Lord's satchel and calls it a purse. He makes the same joke about Alan's satchel in *The Hangover*.

9. *Guardians of the Galaxy* is the first movie in the Marvel Cinematic Universe that was written to be a standalone film, and there are almost zero references to other objects or characters from other movies. Despite this, several characters from *Guardians of the Galaxy* will appear in future Marvel movies with characters from *The Avengers*.

10. Zoe Saldana (Gamora) and Bradley Cooper (Rocket) dated for several years before they accepted roles on the *Guardians of the Galaxy*.

11. Jason Momoa (Khal Drogo on *Game of Thrones*) turned down the role of Drax.

12. In the first draft of the screenplay, Yondu was killed in one of the last scenes of the movie.

13. Olivia Wilde turned down a sizeable offer to play Gamora.

14. In the comic books Drax has green skin, but the producers felt that would confuse the audience into thinking he was the same race as Gamora or a mutant like The Hulk.

15. Star-Lord's ship is inspired by hotrods with large engines. "Its environment is reminiscent of Earth and has a tangible quality - mechanical with chrome and leather and a muscle-car look."

16. Karen Gillan shaved her head as soon as she was offered the role of Nebula.

17. In an interview, Benicio Del Toro described The Collector as "Liberace in outer space."

18. Rocket is director James Gunn's favorite character.

19. Chris Pratt (Star-Lord) and Dave Bautista (Drax) spent nearly three months training and rehearsing for a fight scene together. Three days before they were scheduled to shoot the scene, the sequence was scrapped, and they had to re-learn an entire new one.

20. Gal Gadot auditioned for the role of Nebula but didn't get it. She later landed the role of Wonder Woman in *The Justice League* and *Wonder Woman*.

21. In the comic books, Nebula is Thanos' granddaughter. In the *Guardians of the Galaxy* she is his daughter.

22. Star-Lord's ship is named The Milano after Alyssa Milano, Peter Quill's favorite actress.

23. Director James Gunn handed out containers of Play-Doh to anybody on the set who he felt went above and beyond while filming a scene. When asked why, he said, "I love the smell of Play-Doh. Opening a new container and smelling it puts me in a creative and child-like place. And who doesn't love playing with Play-Doh?"

24. Chris Pratt said his performance was influenced by Han Solo (*Star Wars*) and Marty McFly (*Back to the Future*).

25. Chris Pratt spent six months in intense physical training to prepare for his role. He shed almost 60 pounds in order to look lean and cut for his shirtless scenes.

26. Sales numbers went through the roof for every song that was featured on the soundtrack. It also lead to a buying frenzy on cassette players, which have mostly vanished from modern electronic stores. Fans had to track them down at pawn shops and antique stores.

27. The scene where Star-Lord accidently drops the orb in The Collector's room was not written in the script. But it looked great so they kept it in the movie.

28. Vin Diesel recorded the line, "I am Groot" more than a thousand times and in 15 different languages.

29. Chris Pratt is known for improvising many of his lines, like the one where he says, "If I had a black light, this place would look like a Jackson Pollock painting."

30. After the movie had finished filming, Chris Pratt "liberated" his Star-Lord costume from the movie set in order to visit sick children in the hospital while dressed in his character.

31. Zoe Saldana (Gamora) also played an assassin whose family was murdered in the film *Colombiana*.

32. The mid-credits scene where Groot dances to "I Want You Back" was animated using a cellphone video of director James Gunn dancing as a reference.

Avengers: Age of Ultron (2015)

1. Iron Man's Hulkbuster armor is only referred in the film as "Veronica," and it is only mentioned three times.

2. Ultron's physical design changes throughout the movies, and closely resembles a similar transformation in the comic books. His costume goes from Ultron Mark 1, to Ultron Prime.

3. The Vision's creation was meant to parallel the creation of Frankenstein's Monster. There was controversy surrounding each "monster's" fabrication, and both were brought to life with a blast of lightning.

4. Several Lego block movie tie-in sets were released before the movie arrived in theaters, spoiling several plot points such as the Hulkbuster armor and The Vision. A movie trailer was later released with both of them seen in it.

5. This is the first movie in the Marvel Cinematic Universe to feature The Hulk, but not a scene where he transforms into The Hulk. It does, however, have a scene showing him reverting back into Bruce Banner.

6. In one scene, the main characters are at a party and each of them attempt to lift Thor's hammer, Mjölnir. Steve Rogers (Captain America) is the only one who can make it budge, and you can see the smile on Thor's face vanish. In the comic books, Steve Rogers is one of less than 20 people in the universe who are "worthy" enough to wield the mighty weapon. Black Widow doesn't try to lift the hammer, but is able to lift it in a special comic book series that takes place in an alternate reality.

7. The Hulk has no lines of dialogue in this movie. Bruce Banner has lots to say, but Hulk doesn't say a word, not even "Hulk smash!"

8. In this movie, almost all of the Avenger's team is affected by Scarlet Witch's mind-altering powers. The only Avenger not affected is Hawkeye, who was mind-controlled by Loki for most of *The Avengers*.

9. Ultron's signature line, "There are no strings on me," is from a song in *Pinocchio*, a movie from the 1940s.

10. Special scenes where Iron Man and Captain America argue/fight were written specifically so this movie would connect to *Captain America: Civil War*. Two unique movie posters were also created for *Avengers: Age of Ultron*. One poster shows Iron Man standing in front of Captain America, and the other shows Captain America standing in front of Iron Man.

11. In the comics, The Vision is named by Wasp. In the movies he is named by Thor.

12. Quicksilver and Scarlet Witch are never referred to by their superhero names in *Avengers: Age of Ultron*.

13. Quicksilver is the first "hero" to die in the Marvel Cinematic Universe.

14. Quicksilver's first line of dialogue was, "You didn't see that coming?" and it was also his last line of dialogue. Both lines were spoken to Hawkeye.

15. In the comic books, Ultron is created by Hank Pym (the original Ant-Man) but this was changed so that Ant-Man could have a standalone film before joining the Avengers team.

16. Lindsay Lohan auditioned for the role of Wanda Maximoff (Scarlet Witch).

17. To prepare for her role as Scarlet Witch, Elizabeth Olsen read a lot of comic books. She said in an interview that she was happy her character's costume was drastically changed from the source material, because the comic book costume wouldn't perform well in real-life combat.

18. *Avengers: Age of Ultron* was the first movie to feature Iron Man, but without at least one scene with Pepper Potts.

19. When J.A.R.V.I.S. becomes The Vision, he is replaced by F.R.I.D.A.Y. as in "girl Friday" a slang term from the 1940/50s. A girl Friday was like a secretary who performed small miscellaneous and boring tasks for her boss. The modern-day word would be "gofer."

20. The scenes for Sokovia were shot in a small village in Italy. Italian signs were replaced by ones with the Cyrillic alphabet.

21. When Tony Stark is selecting a new AI, one of the computer chips had "Tadashi" written on it. A reference to *Big Hero 6*, another Marvel movie.

22. In the original draft of the screenplay, Ultron is created by the World Council so they can replace the Avengers, who they believed to be unreliable.

23. The only character in the movie who calls Clint Barton by his superhero name (Hawkeye) is his wife.

24. The first line of dialogue spoken by an Avenger team member is "Shit."

25. In the comic books, Quicksilver and Scarlet Witch are mutants. In the Marvel Cinematic Universe they are regular humans who were enhanced through genetic experiments. This was done to disassociate the "mutant" concept from the MCU.

26. Aaron Taylor-Johnson only accepted the role of Quicksilver because his *Godzilla* co-star (Elizabeth Olsen) accepted the role of Scarlet Witch. They are close friends in real life.

27. James Spader was the only actor to audition for the role of Ultron.

28. Scarlett Johansson was pregnant during the filming of *Avengers: Age of Ultron* and during the later stages of her pregnancy many of her scenes had to be shot with body doubles. A few scenes had to use CGI to replace her belly. Chris Evans said in an interview that the body doubles (when in costume) looked so much like Scarlet Johansson that he would start a conversation with one of them, and only realize halfway through he wasn't talking to Scarlett.

Ant-Man (2015)

1. Cassie's giant ant pet is referred to as a boy. But design of the ant suggests that it is female.

2. Right after Scott Lang escapes prison on the back of the flying ant, he lands on a newspaper. The headline is: "Who is to Blame for Sekovia?" which is a prelude to *Captain America: Civil War*.

3. A flashback scene in Cuba where Hank Pym shrinks a tank was cut from the movie so it would be surprising when a tank is enlarged later in the film.

4. In the movie, Hank Pym sends Scott Lang on an "audition" to earn the Ant-Man suit by performing a heist. In the comics, Scott steals the suit to save his sick daughter and Hank lets him keep it.

5. The producers were only able to use Thomas the Tank Engine's likeness if they agreed the train would remain friendly and not kill anybody.

6. Mary Elizabeth Winstead auditioned to play Janet Van Dyne (The Wasp).

7. The director, Peyton Reed stated in an interview that the main theme of *Ant-Man* was "passing the torch."

8. The original screenplay did not involve The Wasp at all, but she was added so she could be used in future Marvel movies.

9. Adrien Brody, Ewan McGregor, and Joseph Gordon-Levitt all auditioned for the role of Scott Lang.

10. When Paul Rudd informed his nine-year-old son that he was going to play the role of Ant-Man, his son said, "Wow, I can't wait to see how stupid that'll be."

11. Gary Oldman, Pierce Brosnan, and Sean Bean all auditioned for the role of Hank Pym.

12. Craft services served lamb chops for lunch on the same day the scene with the shrunken lamb was shot.

13. When Darren Cross shrinks the board member, causing him to explode, the leftover goop was strawberry jam.

14. Screenwriter Edgar Wright (*Shaun of the Dead, Scott Pilgrim vs. the World*) wanted *Ant-Man* to be a standalone film, but that didn't fit with Marvel's vision and due to creative differences Edgar dropped out of the project after turning in a first draft. Several scenes were used in the final version, but most of it was cut.

15. Jessica Chastain turned down the role of Hope van Dyne.

16. Michael Douglas has asked that the character of his wife (Janet/The Wasp) be played by his real-life wife (Catherine Zeta-Jones) in future movies. Though that might be difficult as she would not have aged normally if she returns from the quantum universe. She'd probably look exactly like she did when she was trapped inside.

17. Steve Buscemi was the first choice to play Hank Pym but he turned down the offer from director Peyton Reed.

18. The first time the character of Ant-Man was seen on screen was in a Saturday Night Live sketch in 1975. The actor who played Ant-Man was Garrett Morris and Garrett has a cameo as a cab driver in *Ant-Man* (2015).

19. In the opening sequence of the film (set in 1989) you can see construction beginning on the S.H.I.E.L.D. headquarters (Triskelion) seen in *Captain America: Winter Soldier*.

20. Michael Douglas accepted the role of Hank Pym so his children could finally watch one of his movies in the theater. (Most of them are rated R.)

21. When Yellowjacket's suit fires a laser beam, it makes the same sound effect as an AT-AT from *Star Wars: The Empire Strikes Back.*

22. Paul Rudd's Ant-Man costume had to be altered because he put on too much muscle while preparing for his role.

23. Michael Douglas turned 70 while shooting Ant-Man. The crew presented him with a cake that looked like a film reel with ants crawling over it.

24. Originally, Marvel wanted the story to focus on Hank Pym, but it was decided that Hank's story wasn't "family friendly" as the character suffered from mental issues and physically abused his wife.

25. Paul Rudd bought an ant farm while preparing for his role as Ant-Man. He liked watching the ants work together to accomplish common goals, and was so inspired by their work ethic that he kept the ant farm even after the movie finished filming.

Captain America: Civil War (2016)

1. The first film in the Marvel Cinematic Universe to feature Spider-Man.

2. The first film to feature Thaddeus Ross but with no scenes from The Hulk.

3. Also the first film to feature Steve Rogers but not Nick Fury.

4. Mark Ruffalo was spotted several times on the set of *Captain America: Civil War* but his scenes were eventually cut from the movie. These scenes will be used in *Thor: Ragnarok*.

5. In the comic books, the mutant factions (X-Men, and the Brotherhood of Mutants) play a large role in the civil war. But since 20th Century Fox owns the film rights to the X-Men franchise, mutants were cut from the film.

6. Thor's clone, Ragnarok, was also a big part of the comic book storyline, but his scenes were cut so they could be later used in *Thor: Ragnarok*.

7. During the fight scene at the airport a stair car (a truck/staircase for helping people onto airplanes) can be seen in the background. The logo on it says: Bluth. This is a reference to *Arrested Development* and is in fact the same stair car used in the TV show. The directors of *Captain America: Civil War* directed several episodes of *Arrested Development* including the pilot.

8. Bucky Barnes has his arm chopped off because Marvel executives wanted to have a scene in every MCU movie where a character loses his hand/arm. This is because one of their favorite movies is *Star Wars: The Empire Strikes Back.* A character loses their hand/arm in almost every Marvel movie.

9. The first time Giant Man has ever been seen on screen.

10. The longest Marvel movie ever created. Running time: 2 hours and 27 minutes.

11. The young Tony Stark seen at the beginning of the film was created entirely with CGI (computer-generated imagery.)

12. This movie is not the first time Marvel has tapped the Civil War storyline outside the comic books. The video game *Ultimate Alliance 2* was also based on fighting surrounding the superhero registry.

13. This is the first film where the Spider-Man special effects were not created by Sony or a Sony-affiliated company.

14. Peter Parker Is wearing a T-Shirt from a pizza delivery place when he meets Tony Stark. In the Spider-Man movies from the 2000s, Peter Parker worked as a pizza delivery driver.

15. In one scene, Tony Stark (Robert Downey Jr.) says how attractive Aunt May (Marisa Tomei) is. Downey and Tomei were in a relationship in the 1990s that lasted several years.

16. The directors cited *Se7en* and *Fargo* as having a heavy influence on this film.

17. Scarlet Witch had a heavy Sokovian accent in *Avengers: Age of Ultron* but the directors asked her to use her normal voice in this film.

18. In each Captain America movie, Steve Rogers has a kissing scene. In *The First Avenger*, he kissed Peggy Carter. In *The Winter Soldier* he kissed Black Widow. In *Civil War* he kisses Sharon Carter.

19. The Vision's clothing was based around popular men's wear from the 1940s and 50s.

20. Tom Holland (Spider-Man) almost broke his nose while doing a flip stunt. He was hurt, but not too hurt to finish filming.

21. The special effect that took the most amount of time and money to create was the computer animation of young Tony Stark at the beginning of the film.

22. This film has spawned thousands of internet memes where Steve Rogers and Tony Stark argue over silly topics. The meme is called: Captain America: Civil War 4 Pane.

23. In the film, Falcon uses a drone called Redwing. In the comics, Redwing was an actual falcon and served as the superhero's sidekick.

24. Many scenes were filmed in May in Atlanta, Georgia. Because of the heat (32°C/90°F) and the heavy costumes, many actors/extras suffered from exhaustion and dehydration.

25. The dark shading around Spider-Man's eyes and the web cartridges on his belt are the only updates Spider-man has had to his costume in decades. His look for this movie was based on his appearance in the 1960s comic books.

26. Tom Holland was chosen as Spider-Man over Charlie Plummer because Charlie was under 18 and the child-labor laws would have limited him to filming only a few hours per day. For *Civil War* this wouldn't have been a problem, but for *Spider-Man: Homecoming* it would have been.

27. Marisa Tomei (age 50) is the youngest woman to portray Aunt May on screen. Rosemary Harris (*Spider-Man 2002*) was in her seventies, and Sally Field (*The Amazing Spider-Man 2012*) was in her sixties. Each woman has been nominated for an Oscar.

28. Chris Evans (Captain America) is always given clothing that is too small by the costume department. This gives him the appearance of having larger muscles.

29. Robert Downey Jr. said he would act in *Civil War* only if his character was given more screen time.

30. This film is a set-up for *Avengers: Infinity War – Part 1* and *Avengers: Infinity War – Part 2*.

31. The first time Black Panther is seen on screen.

32. To prepare for his role as Black Panther, Chadwick Boseman read a ton of Black Panther comic books and even visited South Africa so he could better understand the cultural aspects of the continent.

33. When filming had finished, Sebastian Stan (The Winter Soldier) and Anthony Mackie (Falcon) had a foot race while dressed in full costume.